Thank you to the generous team who gave their time and talents to make this book possible:

Authors
Elizabeth Spor Taylor
Yoseph Ayalew

Illustrator
Alex Regasa

Creative directors
Caroline Kurtz, Jane Kurtz, and Kenny Rasmussen

Translator
Ahmed Dedo Gemeda

Editors
Mastewal Abera and Woubeshet Ayenew

Designer
Beth Crow

Ready Set Go Books, an Open Hearts Big Dreams Project

Copyright © 2022 Ready Set Go Books

ISBN: 979-8839241749
Library of Congress Control Number: 2022912496

All rights reserved. No part of this book may be reproduced, scanned or distributed in any printed or electronic form without permission.
Printed in Seattle, WA, U.S.A.

Publication Date: 08/08/22

I Help

Gargaaru nan jaaladha.

English and Afaan Oromo

I love to help. I help my grandmother fold the clothes.

Gargaaru nan jaaladha. Akkoon koo uffata ishee yommuu dachaaftu nan gargaara.

I help my mother dry the dung we use to cook food and make our house warm.

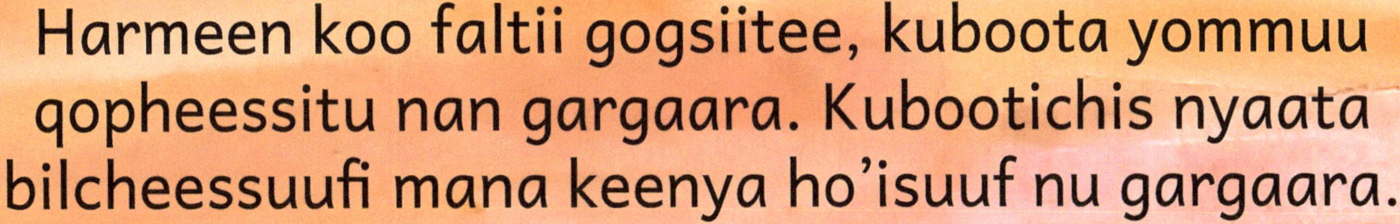

Harmeen koo faltii gogsiitee, kuboota yommuu qopheessitu nan gargaara. Kubootichis nyaata bilcheessuufi mana keenya ho'isuuf nu gargaara.

I help my father wash his feet.

Miila abbaa koo dhiquun abbaa koos nan gargaara.

I help my sister serve the food.

Obboleettiin koo nyaata yommuu dhiyeessitu nan gargaara.

I help my brother care for the cattle.

Loon kunuunsuufi eeguudhaan obboleessa koo nan gargaara.

Sometimes I need help. My grandmother helps me understand the stories she tells.

Yeroo tokko tokko anis gargaarsa nan barbaada. Akkoon koo seenessi ishee akka naaf galu na gargaarti.

My mother helps me when I am ill.

Harmeen koo yommuu na
dhukkubu na kunuunsuun na
gargaarti.

My father helps me get
papers to read in Braille.

Abbaan koo Bireeliin akkan dubbisuuf waraqaa fiduun na gargaara.

My sister helps me get ready for school.

Obboleettiin koo gara mana
barumsaa deemu koo dura
akka qophaa'uuf na gargaarti.

My brother helps me with my schoolwork.

Obboleessi koo hojii mana
barumsaakootiin na gargaara.

My eyes can't see, but my hands can do many things. I help my family. My family helps me. We help each other.

Qaroon ija koo ilaaluu baataniis, harkoonni koo garuu hojiilee baay'ee hojjeechu danda'u. Maatii koo nan gargaara; isaaniis na gargaaru. Nuti hundi walgargaarra.

About the Story

According to the World Health Organization, about six million Ethiopians suffer from blindness or vision loss, well above the world averages. Most of the blindness—more than in any other African country—could have been prevented. The main causes are river blindness, cataracts, measles, vitamin A deficiency and trachoma, which is a disease spread by flies or by sharing cloth.

Even though most blind children in Ethiopia don't get to go to school, a few special education programs are starting to be available. Sebata Blind School in Oromia, for example, provides canes, ramps, slates, stylus, and books in Braille for students. About half the teachers at the school are blind themselves.

A nearby education college trains teachers to help students with special needs. The teachers in training have a chance to work with real students at Sebata Blind School and learn how to educate students in ways that give them a chance to eventually live independent lives. The girl in our story, for example, uses a white cane and reads in Braille, tools that may someday be widespread across Ethiopia.

About The Authors

Elizabeth Spor Taylor is an international literacy specialist who serves as writer and editor of learning materials for Ethiopian children. She has traveled to Ethiopia nearly a dozen times in connection with such work, visiting schools and libraries.

Her expertise is in primary grades literacy relative to native English speakers as well as English Speakers of Other Languages. Elizabeth is currently a Michael Carr's Legacy Project literacy consultant for Open Hearts Big Dreams. She continues to work collaboratively with Ethiopian educators and writers to increase opportunities for all children. Additionally, Elizabeth supports the advancement of adult English skills within the immigrant and refugee population in Cleveland, Ohio.

In addition to writing and doing translation for Open Hearts Big Dreams, Yoseph is a Project Manager for the NGO, leading the printing and distribution of Ready Set Go books in Ethiopia. In fact, in 2022, Yoseph was recognized by OHBD for his dedication to improving literacy in Ethiopia when he received a Literacy Leader Award.

Yoseph has written various children's books in Amharic, English, and Anuak and has also been a teacher for two decades in elementary and middle school. He was one of the founders of MYFV School, which educates children in KG to grade 8, with a goal to include orphans and vulnerable children into the student population. Yoseph has also served as an event planner. For example, he has routinely organized festivals at the Addis Ababa Exhibition Center to celebrate the International Day of African Child. Yoseph also works for Roots Ethiopia as the Partnership and Fundraising Manager.

Outside of the field of education, Yoseph has written and produced ophthalmology bulletins. He is also an insurance agent. His family and friends know him as a solution architect who looks for innovative approaches to problems.

About The Illustrator

Alemayehu "Alex" Regasa was born and lives in Bishoftu, 45 km from the capital city of Addis Ababa, Ethiopia. He says, "I started art by making my handwriting beautiful and copying drawings from history books. I made flowers to give to neighbors on Ethiopian New Year, called Enkutatash. My drawings of flowers were amazing, so neighbors appreciated me. This pushed me to do more art work until I joined Fine Arts and Design University in Addis Ababa."

After graduation he worked in a private studio with friends. Now he does his own art work and gives art workshops for children and sometimes for teachers. He says, "Children are my inspiration because they are free, open minded and honest, so I like to work with them." Alex has exhibited his work at various galleries in Addis Ababa and was a finalist among artists from around the world in an Italian book illustration competition.

About The Inclusivity Consultants

Kirsten Schwabel is an educator of children with significant disabilities. She uses a strength-based approach to meet the individual needs of each child. Her work is done collaboratively, in partnership with families and alongside other professionals. Kirsten is a member of the team creating Ready Set Go books that include, recognize, and celebrate people with disabilities. She lived in Addis Ababa and frequently travels to Ethiopia to continue her work.

Janet Rose was an educator of the Deaf and the Blind for 35 years. She worked as the librarian for the Colorado School for the Deaf and Blind for 27 of those years. Her focus is on making materials interesting and accessible for both populations. She has worked on the Ready Set Go books and curriculum materials, trained teachers and librarians in Ethiopia, and continues to promote libraries, literacy and love of learning.

This hangs in the director's office at Sebata.
http://moscowcoffeereview.com/carpecakem/2016/11/06/visiting-the-school-for-the-blind-in-sebeta-ethiopia/

About Michael Carr's Legacy Project

Disability does not define a life. Mike Carr clearly demonstrated that his life was not defined by his disability. Although Mike was paralyzed at a young age, he still enjoyed a successful career with a high-tech company in Seattle where both his technical skills and leadership were highly valued. Mike was a role model to so many of those he worked with and those who came to know him. He was a strong advocate for the power of inclusion and equal opportunity for individuals with disabilities. The legacy project in his name was created to provide opportunities for children with disabilities in Ethiopia, the birth country of one of his sons. Children with disabilities there do not lack talent or drive. What they too often lack, however, are the tools needed to develop these talents and to apply that drive.

Education remains the key to providing those tools. Unfortunately, educational opportunities for children with disabilities in Ethiopia are rare or in some cases, non-existent. The goal of the legacy project is to increase awareness of the educational disparities of Ethiopian children with disabilities and to increase educational opportunities for these children so they can become the role models of the future that Mike Carr was during his lifetime. Getting to see themselves in our OHBD-RSG is an important step to making this possible.

About Open Hearts Big Dreams

Open Hearts Big Dreams Fund (OHBD) was founded by Ellenore Angelidis, inspired by her Ethiopian born daughter, Leyla Marie Fasika; both are key volunteers. OHBD is a United State 501(c)(3) not-for-profit organization that believes the chance to dream big dreams should not depend on where in the world you are born. Our mission is "Inspiring and empowering youth (K-14) to reimagine their futures by providing literacy, STEAM, and leadership opportunities."

OHBD harnesses the power of collaboration. We are made up of a small number of part-time paid staff and a large number of highly motivated volunteers with advanced skills, including artistic, editorial, translation, and high-tech expertise in Ethiopia, the Diaspora and globally. Our culture of innovation means we act fast on new ideas. Since 2017, we've produced more than 700 bilingual, culturally appropriate early reader titles and a number of STEM and Model programs to increase literacy, inclusion, and leadership.

In Ethiopia, for Ethiopia; OHBD is based in the U.S. but we are committed to working with local content creators and to producing quality books in Ethiopia. Local opportunities and production builds local knowledge and capacity.

About OHBD Ready Set Go Books

Reading has the power to change lives, but many children and adults in Ethiopia cannot read. One reason is that Ethiopia doesn't have enough books in local languages to give people a chance to practice reading. Ready Set Go books wants to close that gap and open a world of ideas and possibilities for kids and their communities.

When you buy an OHBD-RSG book, you provide critical funding to create and distribute more books.

Learn more at: http://openheartsbigdreams.org/book-project/ or find all our books at: https://ohbd-rsgbooks.com

OHBD Proudly Prints in Ethiopia

OHBD developed our own local printing capacity and have a number of our books available to pick up in Addis. They are available for bulk purchase and we regularly donate to schools, libraries and local organizations serving kids. Please contact us at ellenore@openheartsbigdreams.org if interested in samples or ordering.

So far, we have printed and distributed (with collaborating organizations) hundreds of thousands of copies of our books in numerous languages in country.

Our goal is to get these books to all elementary students across Ethiopia.

About the Language

The continent of Africa is home to many people who speak Afaan Oromo. Native speakers of Afaan Oromo, in fact, outnumber speakers of every other language except Arabic, Swahili and Hausa. Most Afaan Oromo speakers live in Ethiopia. (Many also live in the United States.) Using the Latin alphabet for writing Afaan Oromo can be traced back to the nineteenth century but was formally adopted in 1991.

About the Translation

Ahmed Dedo Gemeda is an Assistant Professor of English Language and Literature at Haramaya University. He is currently teaching undergraduate and postgraduate students. He is also serving as a translator, editor and reviewer on academic, technical and literary works.

Over 100+ unique OHBD-RSG books available in nearly 20 languages!

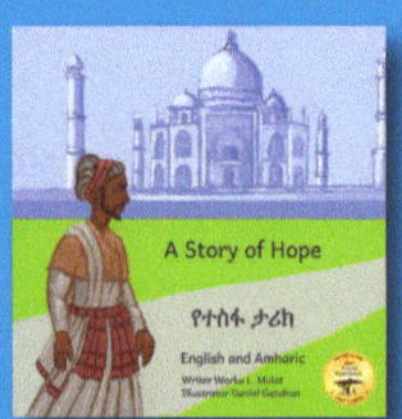

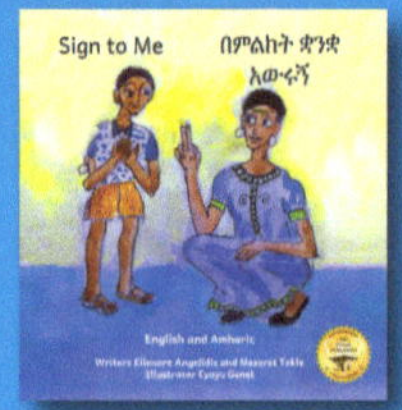

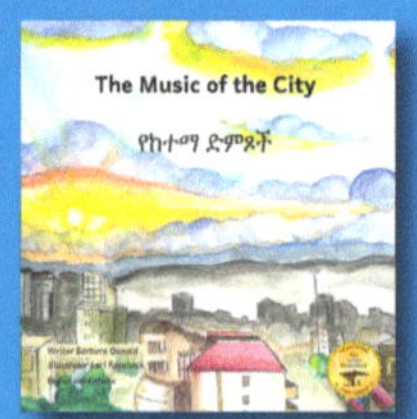

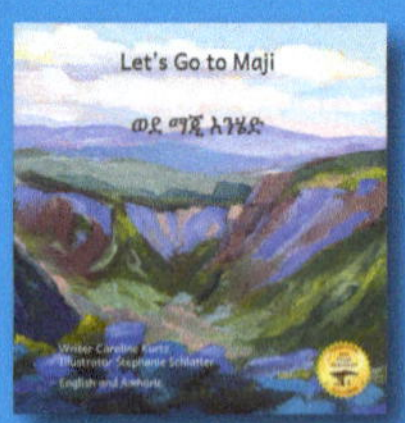

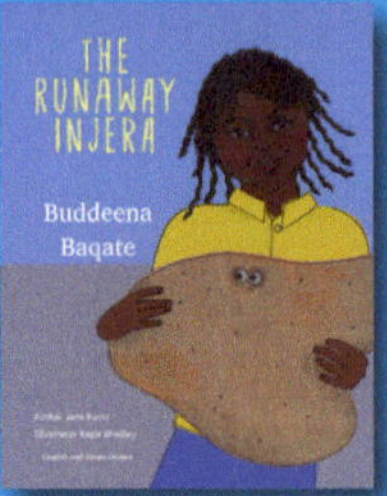

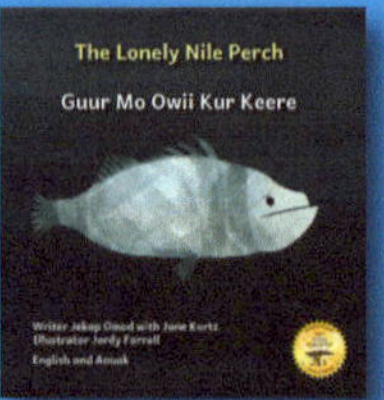

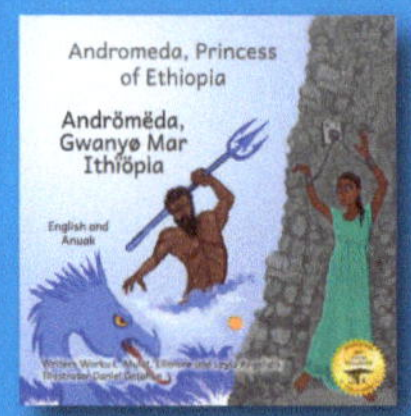

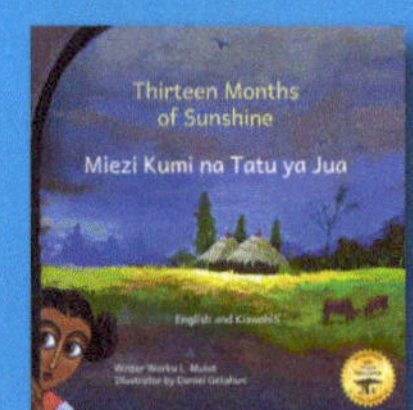

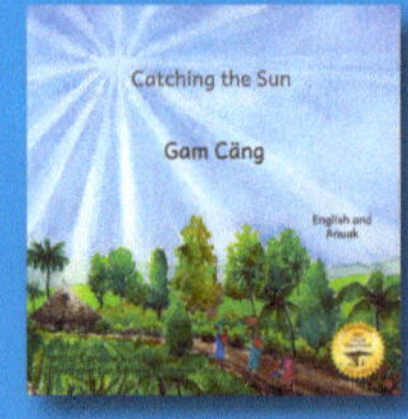

To view all available titles, go to https://ohbd-rsgbooks.com/shop or scan QR code

Open Heart Big Dreams is pleased to offer discounts for bulk orders, educators and organizations.

Contact ellenore@openheartsbigdreams.org for more information.

www.ingramcontent.com/pod-product-compliance
Lightning Source LLC
Chambersburg PA
CBHW042111110726
48006CB00002B/601